What

A book written by

Adam Ahmad Olaitan.

Dedication

This book is dedicated to the unknown love of my life because I have not yet meet her. And to all true lover all over the world.

Acknowledgement

I want to acknowledged first and foremost Almighty Allah who gave me the knowledge to write this book. He is my Lord, my helper and the one who gives me understanding. Without him, I can do nothing.

• What is Love

Love means to be deeply committed and connected to someone or something. Love encompasses a range of strong and positive emotional and mental states, from the most sublime virtue or good habit, the deepest interpersonal affection, to the simplest pleasure.

In simple term, Love is to feel more than liking towards someone. It is a bond that two people share.

• How do I know if I truly love someone

You can know if you are in love if you feel in the following ways :-

1. You prioritize the other person's needs on the same level as your own

When you start thinking about someone else's desires and needs as much as your own, it's a pretty good sign that you are in love, Shaffer says. "You may not necessarily want the same things but when you are in love, you start thinking of the other person's perspective just as much as your own.

2. You feel comfortable being yourself

"When you start allowing your partner to see your flaws, that's when love can flourish,"I believe. You should never feel that you have to hide something from your partner—and if you do, it's probably not real love. That's not to say you should give up on being presentable and polite to your partner, but remember it's often our imperfections and quirks that make us lovable. When you feel comfortable being yourself, for better or worse, that is a good sign that you are in a trusting, loving relationship.

3. You feel grateful for your partner without taking them for granted

If you find yourself feeling thankful for the little things your partner does—not just the grand gestures—then you may be in love

4. You are proud of their accomplishments as if they were your own

When you're in love, you want want to brag about your partner's accomplishments and take pride in their projects, whether they are something you are super interested in or not. Love can be feeling in alignment with your partner's joy and success

5. You are willing to put in the work to understand them even if you have a conflict

Even when you are fighting, love is knowing that you are still on the same team. It can be frustrating but it's worth it to put in the work to peacefully resolve conflicts, which there will be, even and especially when you're in love. Of course it's not fun, but you still want to do it because you want to be with your partner.

6. You feel calm and secure

You should expect to feel some initial nerves when you're getting to know a partner, but eventually they should peter out, and you should feel relaxed around them. After all, your partner is supposed to make you happy and be a positive force in your life. This often means feeling less stressed, more secure, calm, empathetic and trustful."

7. Your feelings for them go beyond physical attraction

Some social scientists describe love as a series of characteristics, according to Francis. "Most notably, Robert Sternberg described love as potentially containing commitment, passion (here meaning physical attraction), and intimacy (meaning emotional connection)." When you're figuring out if you're in love, ask yourself if your feelings encompass all those things—instead of the just the infamous butterflies.

• Is it bad to fall in love

It is bad to love someone. What is bad is to love too much or love the wrong person. These are what could happen to you if you love too much :-

1. You might be too blind to see what's right.

If you love someone too much, your reasoning might be clouded. It will be difficult to see what's right or wrong. For example, you might come to a point in your relationship where you will find emotional and physical abuse okay just because you love your partner. You might even find it acceptable if your partner gets a third party as long as he or she keeps a relationship with you. Being blind because of excessive love can warp your reasoning.

2. If you love someone too much, you might be pouring too much of yourself, too.

If you do, you might be left empty. Remember that a relationship is composed of two complete individuals. If you become incomplete, you will eventually feel like a hole in your life that you do not know how to fill. It will be challenging to love someone because of that.

3. You might make that person you love your world.

It might sound sweet when someone declares that you are his or her world, but don't fall into the trap. Making someone your world will make you lose your identity, and in the end, you will not know yourself anymore. Have you given up on what you want like traveling because your partner is a home buddy? Have you given up on your social life because you want to spend all your time with your partner? Saying yes to the questions may sound sweet, but you should be alarmed if you do. It means you're losing yourself in your relationship.

4. You might neglect yourself.

Have you stopped pampering yourself because you're too busy caring for your partner? Have you stopped looking for self-growth because your only focus is your partner? You might lose the opportunities along the way if you get too busy focusing on the one you love. Neglecting yourself because of too much love for your partner might backfire and make you feel you have not made much of your life. It might also make you feel too tired. Who knows? You might wake up one day feeling that you can't give any more love.

5. You might lose time with your friends.

Ditcher. That's your friend who ditched you when he or she got into a relationship. That might also be you if you just have abandoned your friends because of too much love for your partner. Friends aren't just a part of a specific phase in your life, so you shouldn't be ditching them so that you can spend all the time you have with your partner. Remember that your friends have been with you through thick and thin before you got to know your partner. Is it really right to just abandon them?

6. You might have no time to spare for your family.

Have you been missing out on important family gatherings? Has it been ages since you last ate dinner with your family? Unfortunately, loving someone too much might take even the time you spend with your family.

7. You might lose track of reality.

Because you love someone too much, you might have let some crucial standards and deal breakers go. For example, you two have different religious beliefs. You might also be in a constant fight with each other because of irreconcilable differences. However, you don't mind them as long as you can keep the relationship because of too much love. You might have chosen not to see that the relationship isn't going anywhere because of too much love.

8. You might develop an unhealthy dependency.

Can you still drive yourself home the way you did before? Can you still buy the groceries on your own? Those are simple things you can do on your own before but might not do now because you have depended too much on your partner. We do not want to think of the worst, but if you lose your partner, can you still live independently or will you be left paralyzed?

9. Your partner might find you smothering.

Loving someone too much may lead you to be excessively clingy. You might not want your partner to be with anyone else but you. You might get jealous of his friends, officemates, or even his parents if he spends time with them. You might tend to force your partner to cut all his ties with other people so that you can be sure he or she is yours and yours alone. The possible result? Your partner is smothered and wants to run away from you.

10. Your too much love can make your partner complacent.

Or worse, your partner might take you for granted. He or she might be aware that you give too much love and might take advantage of it. He or she knows you'll forgive him or her if he or she does something wrong, so he or she might not think twice of his or her actions. As a result, he might not exert effort in making your relationship work and leave everything on your shoulders.

11. You might feel dissatisfied with your partner.

Because you give too much love, you might expect that your partner will do the same. If you've given up your social life for him or her, you might expect him or her to do the same. If you've let opportunities pass for him or her, you might expcct the same. As a result, you will feel uncontented.

So you see, anything in excess is detrimental. Love isn't an exception. Loving someone too much is dangerous for you, your partner, and your relationship. Keep things regulated, so you can keep things right.

• How do you know if you are experiencing a true love

1. Hurt and Annoyance

You become very hurt when your partner annoys you; however, what they do never makes you mad. You might at times become irritated for a moment but you are simply unable to remain mad at them for a long time. You avoid giving them 'nil by mouth' as this is more hurting for you.

2. The Appropriate Endeavor

You go the extra mile to make the relationship work and consciously put in effort to make your loved one happy and give them a feeling of being special and loved.

3. You Avoid Inflicting Pain

When you really love a person, it is hard for you to picture inflicting either emotional or physical pain. Revenge is a powerful human urge; however, true love renders you totally selfless.

4. You Are a Person of Your Word

You keep your promises to your loved one, even if they are not in a position to know whether you broke it.

Love makes you develop an extremely powerful moral conscience in regard to this exceptional individual.

5. It's only "We"

In an ideal relationship, having your personal space to develop personally is advisable.

Regardless, if you genuinely love your partner, you view them as a section of your life. When you make plans for your future, you include them.

6. Being Inseparable

You derive pleasure from being in each other's company in a homely environment. You are truly 'at home' with each other. When together, time literally seems to fly and you cannot wait until the next time to meet; you literally count the hours!

7. Being Open with One Another

When together, you can talk about anything and there is no pretense. A person you love is one you can be yourself with and open up on any subject. You confide what is in your heart and mind, without restraint.

8. Caring Attitude

You are affectionate, cordial and flexible with each other. The two of you anticipate the finest from each other.

You treat one another with utmost care, putting the other person's needs before yours.

9. Ability to Resolve Issues

Compared to a lot of other couples, you have extra ability to solve problems which others find hard to deal with.

You manage to ensure that rather that break you, these experiences make you stronger in your relationship.

10. Supporting Each Other

There exists a mutual feeling of development and support of each other. You both offer one another growing space so as to become independent individuals. This entails encouraging one another in life goals and objectives.

11. Giving One Another Priority

You each have your personal friends and interests. However, giving your partner priority over these things indicates that you love them.

This shows your commitment and is a sign to your partner that they are the most important aspect of your life.

12. Actions Really Do Speak Louder!

A loved one's actions are the most expressive in terms of love. Your partner speaks and puts into action whatever they promise to.

A declaration of love should be accompanied by actions, to support this as true.

13. Making Sacrifices

Your partner might love a game which you do not find interesting at all. However, as they desire your company, you agree to accompany them to watch this game. This is because you are concerned about their happiness and are willing to sacrifice your feelings for them.

14. Surprising Each Other

When you love a person, you enjoy giving them surprises such as gifts and treats. This indicates that you are on their mind all the time and the sight of something pleasing just triggers you into action and you buy it and present it at a time they least expect it.

The element of surprise and joy on their face is truly a gift to you as well!

15. You are Known to Your Partner's Friends and Family

True love does not entail any secrets. The two of you introduce each other to your respective friends and family.

This shows you desire your partner to be accepted by your close ones and become a huge part of your life. This is an indication that you consider the relationship serious and that it is headed somewhere.

In case a loved one is hesitant to let you meet friends and family, this might be an indication that there is a part of their life they want to keep away from you.

You should know that true love means warmth, tenderness, passion, desire, and a sentiment that is unconditional, regardless of good times or hardships.

• Differences between love and attraction

The following are the signs that you are just attached and not in love with someone:-

1. Attachment makes you selfish

When you're in love, you'll be selfless, but attachment makes you selfish. If you're in love with him, you'll try your best to see him happy. You'll also make him know you care and want to meet his needs. True love won't allow you to manipulate, follow or force him into things he doesn't like.

2. You don't care about his feelings

However, if you're just attached to him, you'll not care much about his feelings. Instead, you'll want him to be doing things that only make you happy. In some instances, you'll force him to do whatever pleases you without bothering about how he'll feel afterward.

3. You want to control him

When you're attached to him, you will quickly get angry if he doesn't meet your expectations, something that's so selfish. If you love him, you'll not control him, but attachment does that. When you love him, you'll be yourself and be free with one another. You will strive to make him better, wish to see him prosper in life, and be his protector.

4. Loving means trust

Loving him will make you develop trust and work for your success in the relationship. With attachment, all you'll care about is if he does what you want every time. Without him meeting your demands, you'll mostly be looking for other options to force him into your ways. If he's a social being with many friends, you'll find ways to separate him from them.

You'll either cite insecurity or lack of enough time together. Being attached to him may also make you do things you'd never do to any man in your rightful senses. For example, forcing him to spend most of his time with you when he doesn't want to do so.

5. Love has no time limit, while attachment has a time limitation

If you love him, you'll never be in a rush to either formalize your relationship or make people know about it. You'll want to take your time to learn more about him, even if he's your childhood friend. If you love him, you'll also take your time to emotionally get attached to him, allow him to prepare adequately financially before getting married or engaged.

However, the attachment will make you force things even when it seems not to be working out. All you want to do is have him around you, even in the odd hours, without considering how he feels.

6. Love comes with challenges, but when you're attached, you'll rarely see that

If you love him, you'll fight, separate, reconcile, and get together as if nothing happened. You will also work to see both of you succeed in your relationship, no matter where you're. If it's a long-distance relationship, you'll ensure you stay loyal to him and bear all the challenges that come with it.

However, if you're just attached to him, you'll only see the pinch when you're not together. Your primary target will be how many times you see him and not strive to grow your relationship. You'll never have a long-term goal with him since you're not in love; hence no challenges. The relationship will be more about how you'll feel and not what he sees about the matter.

7. Love is a mutual feeling, but being attached is forcing things your way

If you love him, he should also reciprocate with no second thought. Love will make both of you work towards a common goal and want to see either of the partners succeed. By loving him, you understand that two are better than one. You'll also know that there are things you can't achieve without him.

But if you're attached to him, you'll never bother whether the relationship leads nowhere or if he's unhappy. You will mostly not resolve serious matters since that's not your main concern. Being attached can make you expect him to have no mistakes. But you'll not allow him to mention any of your weaknesses. With such an attitude, you'll not be able to work as a team but rather compete with him.

8. If you love him, the feeling will never change, but being attached is just for some time

If you love your partner, you'll never forget about him, even if you separate for years. For you, he's the only man you'll truly understand and care for.

You will do everything within your means to have him back and, if not, cherish him secretly. If you never get the chance to get back together after a breakup, you'll wish him well in his endeavors.

But if you are just attached to him, you'll be a bitter person after breaking up. To you, he'll have betrayed your trust and even curse him. Attachment can make you plan revenge since you're disappointed with him for not maintaining your happiness. If you move on from the attachment, you'll never want anything to do with him and even assume he never existed in your life.

9. You need communication when you're in love

Although there's a need for constant communication when you're in love, attachment makes you do it to the extreme. If you're attached to him, you'll want to communicate throughout the day without a break which is unhealthy.

10. You don't give him personal space

If you genuinely love him, you'll give him personal space, which will also spice up the relationship. You'll not want to expose him to different people, call or text too much, or spend most of your time together. But being attached will make you prove points that are irrelevant to him.

11. You can't trust him

Being attached makes you a jealous partner who can't trust him with anyone. You'll likely live in fear of losing him to your friends or any girl around him. Jealousy can make you possessive and control a man while not loving him.

12. You are stuck to old practices

Being attached can make you stick to old practices, which may not allow your relationship to blossom. You will see everything to be okay even when all is breaking apart.

13. You expect more than you'll offer

If you're attached, you expect him to give you more than you'll offer. To you, the advantages of having him in your life are more significant than your commitment.

14. You lose your identity

You lose your identity if you're attached to him since you believe there's nothing you can do without him. All you'll do is follow him blindly and, at times, fail to question him when he's wrong for fear of losing him.

15. Looking to validate your feelings for him

If you like posting him to your social media accounts or introducing him to your friends, know it's an attachment. All you're trying to do is validate your feelings for him and set boundaries with your competitors.

• Factors that help you find true love

Humans weren't designed to be alone. Our DNA codes are designed to seek out a mate and continue the human race. No pressure. Before you can take on the challenges of keeping the planet populated, you have to fall in love. Easier said than done, right? Actually, it can be easy when you open yourself up to the possibilities. Are you ready to find love? These following tips can help put you on the path:-

#1: Know What You're Looking For

To merely say out loud, "I want to be in love with someone nice" is a good start but way too vague. You have to know what you're looking for and apply that to your quest to find love. For instance, if you want to be in a long-term committed relationship, then a "one-night stand" should be off the table regardless of how tempted you might be.

It sends the wrong signals. It might help to write down all the qualities you're looking for in a prospective love interest. The person you find might not "check off" all the items but they should be close enough to insure happiness.

#2: Embrace Your Awesomeness

Just as you're going to write out a list of the qualities you want in a partner, you should also write out a list of what you have to offer. Your own awesomeness should not be overlooked. A lot of this has to do with confidence building.

If the person you're seeking out can't appreciate all you have to give, then perhaps they aren't worthy of being on the receiving end of those gifts.

#3: Dive into the Online Dating World

According to surveys, up to 84% of people who are using online dating sites are doing so to find love in a romantic relationship and not just a quick "hook up." That bodes well for your potential search because it means that a majority of the possible dates you'll run across are looking for the same thing that you are.

It is always good to build a relationship on common ground. As intimidating as online dating might appear, it is the best place to meet a wide variety of potential dates all from the comfort of your own laptop.

#4: Consider a Blast from the Past

Is there anyone in your past that you still think of today? Perhaps you both hit it off but were in the wrong place for a commitment. Maybe you were coming out of a bad breakup and weren't ready to be with anyone.

Maybe it is time to revisit your past and see if there might be a connection to rekindle.

#5: Expand Your Social Network

There is nothing wrong with having a tight group of friends that you can rely on. Unfortunately, sticking with that tight group might not open yourself up to the possibilities of finding a new love. By now, your good friends have probably already fixed you up with all their single friends. If it didn't work, then the dating pool is closed.

Consider signing up for a class or workshop on a topic that interests you. Accept an invitation to a social gathering that you might not have readily considered before. The goal is to expand your social network to increase your chances of meeting someone new.

#6: Ask Out Your Crush

It might be someone you work with. It might be the barista you get coffee from each morning. It could be a fellow dog owner you see at the park. If you're single, then you probably have a few crushes tucked away. Work up the courage and ask them out.

The worst that can happen is that they say no and you move on. At least that way, you can take them off the list.

#7: Work on Your Social Game

To find love is to go on a date. Maybe a lot of dates. If it has been awhile since your last date, then your social game might be a little rusty. You can work on your social game by engaging in conversations with random folks you meet throughout the day.

Talk to the cashier at the grocery store or the server at the café. If you're stuck in a line, then you have a perfect opportunity for a chat. This will make it more comfortable to engage in conversation with the next date.

• Why do we fall in love

Love they say is a beautiful thing. The intertwining of two souls, an unexplainable rush of feelings towards someone. Whatever way it makes you feel or act, love grows, and there are a series of events that ultimately lead people to fall in love.

Unlike most other phenomenon in life, love has no definite cause and can be triggered by uncanny of circumstances, events and occurrences. Over the years, science has shed light on the cause and process of falling in love, the chemical involved such as Dopamine, Oxytocin, Norepinephrine and Phenylethylamine, Testosterone and the rest of it.

But then, love isn't just about some chemicals, it's a function of preference and personal history.

Here are some factors that contribute to what makes people fall in love.

1. The way they smell

Smells are emotional triggers. They trigger emotions built up from memories of the person you know. I once had an ex who used a particular perfume, when the relationship went southwards and we parted ways, I met an awesome guy but quickly disliked him because he used the same perfume as my ex.

This scenario also works the other way round, when you've been in a relationship or dating someone for a very long time, you master how they smell. "I miss your fragrance, sometimes I miss it this much that I can clearly smell you in the air." — Qaisar Iqbal Janjua.

This explains why couples cling to each other's clothing and personal items when the other is far away, thy reconnect memories of their lovers through a whiff of the characteristic smell.

2. Similarities

You tend to fall in love with someone who has similar traits and interests as you, share your love for art, music, food or any other thing. I have always seen similarities as the primary cause of people falling in love. I once had a friend Jeff who loved to paint water lilies, he would sit for hours by the sides, coloring these magnificent plants.

Unfortunately, his art seemingly made it impossible to keep any relationship going as most women he met complained he seldom gave them enough attention nor spent substantial time with them until he met Lisa. Lisa was an art major, and the moment the two met, it was like a match made in watercolor heaven.

The similarity of interest is indeed a major factor that influences who you fall in love with.

3. Physical characteristics

We've heard of people drooling over actors and fitness models. Physical characteristic since the ancient times has been a contributing factor in falling in love. The reason is not far-fetched, the general attraction to a person is primarily focused on the outer physical appearance.

Firstly, a term most prefer to call 'infatuation.' Whichever the case, physical characteristics such as beauty, height, smile, and color of the eyes, sure contributes to what makes you fall in love with someone.

4. Laughter

The way a person laughs could trigger emotions and prompt you to fall in love. Laughter plays an important role in any relationship, and sometimes you realize you may start to laugh like the person you are in a relationship with.

Suddenly you love the sound of their laughter so much that you subconsciously begin to mimic their own style of laughter, and trust me it is perfectly natural. Many don't realize this, but when you fall in love with someone, you tend to borrow their body language and speech pattern, it's not awkward there's a scientific explanation to it.

"A smile is the light in your window that tells others that there is a caring, sharing person inside," Denis Waitley.

5. When they make you feel safe

Care, affection, attention, these are attributes of love. When a person makes you feel safe through constant care, affection and concern, you are bound to develop feelings for him/her. Human beings are social animals, and as such you are easily attracted to people who show you care, attention and affection.

Nick Cannon once said, "I think one of the most important things in a relationship is caring for your significant other through good times and bad." When someone cares about you, you feel safe around them and ultimately fall in-love with them.

6. To grow beyond ourselves

A psychologist at UCLA Martie Haselton believes love is a "commitment device," a means by which two human beings encourage themselves to form lasting bonds through sharing of traits that promote personal development.

Another study conducted by Arthur Aron a psychologist at Stony Brook University suggests that the basic instinct of a human being is to "expand the self and to increase our abilities and our effectiveness." Learning one or two from a person can trigger emotions which may ultimately lead to true love.

In conclusion, there is no definite pattern to falling in love, it could happen with anyone, anyway and at any given circumstance.

• Is love a distraction

To someone, it is. To another, it is not. It all depends on how you love. For instance, is love of your parents a distraction? Is your love for your siblings a distraction?.

Just like I said earlier, fake love causes distraction, hurts you. Therefore terminate the relationship you noticed your partner doesn't love you truly.

With everything I said above, I hope you find the answers to your question. If not, you can contact me by sending an email to 'youngengineer1010@gmail.com' . I will be happy to answer your question.

Written by

Adam Ahmad Olaitan

(Robotfee)

I dedicated this write up to the future love of my life. I pray we meet ourselves soon.

Thanks for reading.